TRADITIONAL AUSTRIAN COOKBOOK

AVA BAKER

TRADITIONAL AUSTRIAN COOKBOOK

Copyright © 2024 Ava Baker

All rights reserved.

CONTENTS

APPETIZERS AND SNACKS 1

Wiener Schnitzel Bites 1
Käsespätzle (Cheese Noodles) 3
Gebackener Camembert (Fried Camembert) 5
Kartoffelpuffer (Potato Pancakes) 6
Marillenknödel (Apricot Dumplings) 8
Krautfleckerl (Cabbage Pasta) 10
Liptauer Spread 11
Erdäpfelsalat (Potato Salad) 12
Griessnockerlsuppe (Semolina Dumpling Soup) 13
Räucherlachsrolle (Smoked Salmon Roll) 15

SOUPS AND STEWS 17

Gulaschsuppe (Goulash Soup) 17
Frittatensuppe (Pancake Strip Soup) 19
Leberknödelsuppe (Liver Dumpling Soup) 21
Kürbiscremesuppe (Pumpkin Cream Soup) 23
Krautsuppe (Cabbage Soup) 25
Steirische Eierschwammerlsuppe (Styrian Chanterelle Soup) 27
Würstelgulasch (Sausage Goulash) 29
Grammelknödel Suppe (Crackling Dumpling Soup) 31
Rindsuppe mit Frittaten (Beef Broth with Pancakes) 33
Karfiolcremesuppe (Cauliflower Cream Soup) 35

MAIN COURSES - MEAT DISHES 37

Wiener Schnitzel	37
Tafelspitz (Boiled Beef)	39
Schweinsbraten (Roast Pork)	41
Beuschel (Tripe Stew)	43
Hühnerfrikassee (Chicken Fricassee)	45
Zwiebelrostbraten (Onion Roast Beef)	47
Leberkäse (Liver Cheese)	49
Geselchtes mit Sauerkraut (Smoked Meat with Sauerkraut)	51
Rindsrouladen (Beef Rouladen)	53
Blunzengröstl (Blood Sausage Hash)	55

MAIN COURSES - VEGETARIAN DISHES   56

Kasnocken (Cheese Dumplings)	56
Spinatknödel (Spinach Dumplings)	58
Schwammerlgulasch (Mushroom Goulash)	60
Käsekrainer mit Sauerkraut (Cheese-filled Sausages with Sauerkraut)	62
Erdäpfelgulasch (Potato Goulash)	64
Gemüsestrudel (Vegetable Strudel)	66
Kürbisrisotto (Pumpkin Risotto)	69
Topfenknödel (Quark Dumplings)	71
Krautfleisch (Cabbage and Meat Stew)	73
Linsen mit Knödel (Lentils with Dumplings)	75

DESSERTS AND PASTRIES   77

Apfelstrudel (Apple Strudel)	77
Sachertorte (Sacher Cake)	80
Topfenstrudel (Quark Strudel)	83
Kaiserschmarrn (Emperor's Pancake)	85
Dobostorte (Dobos Cake)	87

LINZER TORTE	90
MOHR IM HEMD (CHOCOLATE PUDDING WITH WHIPPED CREAM)	92
NUSSKIPFERL (NUT CRESCENTS)	94
BUCHTELN (SWEET YEAST DUMPLINGS)	96
ESTERHÁZYTORTE (ESTERHÁZY CAKE)	98

MEASURES 101

TRADITIONAL AUSTRIAN COOKBOOK

APPETIZERS AND SNACKS

Wiener Schnitzel Bites

Servings: 4

Time: 30 minutes

Ingredients:

- 1 pound veal or pork, thinly sliced
- Salt and pepper to taste
- 1 cup all-purpose flour
- 2 eggs, beaten
- 1 cup breadcrumbs
- Oil for frying
- Lemon wedges for serving

Directions:

1. Season the veal or pork slices with salt and pepper.
2. Dredge each slice in flour, dip into beaten eggs, then coat with breadcrumbs.
3. Heat oil in a pan over medium heat. Fry the coated slices until golden brown and crispy.
4. Place the Schnitzel Bites on a paper towel to absorb excess oil.
5. Serve hot with lemon wedges on the side.

Käsespätzle (Cheese Noodles)

Servings: 4

Time: 45 minutes

Ingredients:

- 2 cups all-purpose flour
- 4 large eggs
- 1/2 cup whole milk
- Salt to taste
- 1 cup grated Emmental or Gruyère cheese
- 1 large onion, thinly sliced
- 3 tablespoons butter
- Freshly ground black pepper

Directions:

1. In a bowl, whisk together flour, eggs, milk, and a pinch of salt to form a thick batter.
2. Boil salted water in a large pot. Using a spatula, press the batter through a spätzle maker or a colander into the boiling water.
3. Cook the spätzle for 2-3 minutes or until they float. Drain and set aside.
4. In a pan, sauté sliced onions in butter until golden brown.

5. Add the cooked spätzle to the pan, mixing well with the onions.
6. Sprinkle grated cheese over the spätzle and stir until the cheese melts.
7. Season with salt and pepper to taste.

Gebackener Camembert (Fried Camembert)

Servings: 4

Time: 20 minutes

Ingredients:

- 1 round of Camembert cheese
- 1 cup breadcrumbs
- 2 eggs, beaten
- 1/2 cup all-purpose flour
- Oil for frying
- Cranberry sauce for dipping (optional)

Directions:

1. Cut the Camembert into wedges or cubes.
2. Dredge each wedge in flour, dip into beaten eggs, then coat with breadcrumbs.
3. Heat oil in a pan over medium heat.
4. Fry the Camembert wedges until golden brown on all sides.
5. Place on a paper towel to absorb excess oil.
6. Serve hot with cranberry sauce for a delightful dipping experience.

Kartoffelpuffer (Potato Pancakes)

Servings: 4

Time: 30 minutes

Ingredients:

- 4 large potatoes, peeled and grated
- 1 small onion, finely chopped
- 2 eggs, beaten
- 3 tablespoons all-purpose flour
- 1 teaspoon salt
- 1/2 teaspoon black pepper
- Vegetable oil for frying
- Sour cream or applesauce for serving

Directions:

1. Grate the peeled potatoes using a box grater.
2. Place the grated potatoes in a clean kitchen towel and squeeze out excess moisture.
3. In a bowl, mix grated potatoes, chopped onion, beaten eggs, flour, salt, and black pepper.
4. Heat vegetable oil in a pan over medium heat.
5. Spoon portions of the potato mixture into the hot oil, flattening each with a spatula.

6. Fry until golden brown on both sides, about 3-4 minutes per side.
7. Place on a paper towel to absorb excess oil.
8. Serve hot with a side of sour cream or applesauce.

Marillenknödel (Apricot Dumplings)

Servings: 4

Time: 45 minutes

Ingredients:

- 8 large apricots, pitted
- 1 cup mashed potatoes
- 1 cup all-purpose flour
- 1 egg
- Pinch of salt
- 8 sugar cubes
- Buttered breadcrumbs for coating
- Powdered sugar for dusting

Directions:

1. Boil the potatoes, mash them, and let them cool.
2. Mix mashed potatoes, flour, egg, and a pinch of salt to form a dough.
3. Divide the dough into 8 portions.
4. Flatten each dough portion and encase a pitted apricot and a sugar cube inside.
5. Seal the dumplings, ensuring the apricot is completely covered.

6. Carefully drop the dumplings into boiling water and simmer until they float to the surface.
7. In a separate pan, toast breadcrumbs in butter until golden brown.
8. Roll the boiled dumplings in buttered breadcrumbs.
9. Dust with powdered sugar before serving.

Krautfleckerl (Cabbage Pasta)

Servings: 4

Time: 40 minutes

Ingredients:

- 8 oz (about 250g) egg noodles or short pasta
- 1/2 small cabbage, finely shredded
- 1 onion, finely chopped
- 2 tablespoons vegetable oil
- 1 teaspoon caraway seeds
- Salt and pepper to taste
- Chopped fresh parsley for garnish

Directions:

1. Cook the egg noodles or pasta according to package instructions. Drain and set aside.
2. In a large pan, heat vegetable oil over medium heat.
3. Add chopped onions and sauté until translucent.
4. Stir in caraway seeds and shredded cabbage. Cook until the cabbage is tender.
5. Season with salt and pepper to taste.
6. Add the cooked noodles or pasta to the cabbage mixture, tossing to combine.

7. Cook for an additional 2-3 minutes to let the flavors meld.
8. Garnish with chopped fresh parsley before serving.

Liptauer Spread

Servings: 8

Time: 15 minutes

Ingredients:

- 1 cup soft cream cheese
- 2 tablespoons unsalted butter, softened
- 2 teaspoons sweet paprika
- 1 teaspoon caraway seeds, crushed
- 1 small onion, finely grated
- 2 tablespoons capers, drained and chopped
- 2 teaspoons Dijon mustard
- Salt and pepper to taste
- Chopped chives for garnish

Directions:

1. In a bowl, combine cream cheese and softened butter until smooth.
2. Mix in sweet paprika, crushed caraway seeds, grated onion, chopped capers, and Dijon mustard.
3. Season with salt and pepper to taste. Adjust paprika for color and flavor.
4. Chill the spread in the refrigerator for at least 1 hour.
5. Before serving, garnish with chopped chives.

6. Serve with fresh bread or crackers.

Erdäpfelsalat (Potato Salad)

Servings: 4

Time: 30 minutes

Ingredients:

- 1 1/2 lbs (about 700g) waxy potatoes, boiled and diced
- 1 small red onion, finely chopped
- 3 tablespoons vegetable oil
- 2 tablespoons white wine vinegar
- 1 teaspoon Dijon mustard
- Salt and pepper to taste
- Fresh chives for garnish

Directions:

1. Boil the potatoes until tender. Allow them to cool and then dice into bite-sized pieces.
2. In a large bowl, combine diced potatoes and finely chopped red onion.
3. In a separate bowl, whisk together vegetable oil, white wine vinegar, Dijon mustard, salt, and pepper.
4. Pour the dressing over the potatoes and toss gently to coat evenly.
5. Allow the Erdäpfelsalat to marinate for at least 15 minutes.

6. Garnish with fresh chives before serving.

Grießnockerlsuppe (Semolina Dumpling Soup)

Servings: 4

Time: 30 minutes

Ingredients:

For the Semolina Dumplings:

- 1/2 cup semolina
- 1/4 cup all-purpose flour
- 1/2 teaspoon salt
- 1/4 teaspoon ground nutmeg
- 2 large eggs
- 2 tablespoons milk

For the Soup:

- 6 cups clear vegetable or chicken broth
- 1 carrot, peeled and diced
- 1 celery stalk, diced
- 1 leek, sliced
- 2 tablespoons butter
- Salt and pepper to taste
- Chopped fresh parsley for garnish

Directions:

For the Semolina Dumplings:

1. In a bowl, mix semolina, flour, salt, and ground nutmeg.
2. In a separate bowl, whisk together eggs and milk.
3. Combine the wet and dry ingredients, stirring until well mixed.
4. Let the batter rest for 10 minutes.

For the Soup:

1. In a pot, sauté diced carrot, celery, and leek in butter until softened.
2. Pour in the clear vegetable or chicken broth and bring it to a gentle simmer.
3. Using two teaspoons, form small dumplings from the semolina batter and gently drop them into the simmering broth.
4. Cook the dumplings for about 8-10 minutes or until they float to the surface.
5. Season the soup with salt and pepper to taste.
6. Garnish with chopped fresh parsley before serving.

Räucherlachsrolle (Smoked Salmon Roll)

Servings: 6

Time: 20 minutes

Ingredients:

- 8 oz (about 225g) smoked salmon slices
- 8 oz cream cheese, softened
- 1 tablespoon fresh dill, chopped
- 1 tablespoon capers, drained
- 1 tablespoon red onion, finely chopped
- 1 teaspoon Dijon mustard
- Freshly ground black pepper
- Lemon wedges for serving
- Fresh dill sprigs for garnish

Directions:

1. Lay out the smoked salmon slices on a clean surface, slightly overlapping.
2. In a bowl, mix softened cream cheese, chopped fresh dill, capers, chopped red onion, Dijon mustard, and black pepper.
3. Spread the cream cheese mixture evenly over the smoked salmon.
4. Carefully roll the salmon into a log shape.

5. Wrap the roll in plastic wrap and refrigerate for at least 1 hour to set.
6. Before serving, unwrap the roll and slice into rounds.
7. Arrange on a platter, garnish with fresh dill sprigs, and serve with lemon wedges on the side.

SOUPS AND STEWS

Gulaschsuppe (Goulash Soup)

Servings: 6

Time: 1 hour 30 minutes

Ingredients:

- 1.5 lbs (about 700g) beef stew meat, cubed
- 2 tablespoons vegetable oil
- 2 large onions, finely chopped
- 2 cloves garlic, minced
- 2 tablespoons sweet paprika
- 1 teaspoon caraway seeds
- 2 tablespoons tomato paste
- 1 large potato, peeled and diced

- 1 large carrot, peeled and sliced
- 1 red bell pepper, diced
- 6 cups beef broth
- Salt and pepper to taste
- Chopped fresh parsley for garnish

Directions:

1. In a large pot, heat vegetable oil over medium-high heat. Brown the beef cubes on all sides. Remove and set aside.
2. In the same pot, add chopped onions and garlic. Sauté until softened.
3. Stir in sweet paprika, caraway seeds, and tomato paste. Cook for 2 minutes.
4. Return the browned beef to the pot, and add diced potatoes, sliced carrots, and diced red bell pepper.
5. Pour in beef broth, ensuring all ingredients are submerged. Bring to a boil.
6. Reduce heat to low, cover, and simmer for 1 hour or until the meat is tender.
7. Season with salt and pepper to taste.
8. Garnish with chopped fresh parsley before serving.

Frittatensuppe (Pancake Strip Soup)

Servings: 4

Time: 30 minutes

Ingredients:

For the Pancake Strips:

- **1 cup all-purpose flour**
- **2 eggs**
- **1 cup milk**
- **Salt and pepper to taste**
- **2 tablespoons vegetable oil**

For the Soup:

- **6 cups clear beef or vegetable broth**
- **1 carrot, julienned**
- **1 leek, sliced**
- **2 tablespoons butter**
- **Salt and pepper to taste**
- **Chopped fresh chives for garnish**

Directions:

For the Pancake Strips:

1. In a bowl, whisk together flour, eggs, milk, salt, and pepper to form a smooth batter.

2. Heat vegetable oil in a pan over medium heat.
3. Pour a thin layer of the batter into the pan, swirling to coat the bottom.
4. Cook each side of the pancake for 1-2 minutes or until lightly browned. Repeat until all batter is used.
5. Let the pancakes cool and then roll them up. Slice into thin strips.

For the Soup:

1. In a pot, sauté julienned carrot and sliced leek in butter until softened.
2. Pour in the clear beef or vegetable broth and bring it to a gentle simmer.
3. Season with salt and pepper to taste.
4. Add the sliced pancake strips to the simmering broth.
5. Cook for an additional 2-3 minutes until the strips are heated through.
6. Garnish with chopped fresh chives before serving.

Leberknödelsuppe (Liver Dumpling Soup)

Servings: 4

Time: 45 minutes

Ingredients:

For the Liver Dumplings:

- 1/2 lb (about 225g) chicken or pork liver, finely chopped
- 1/2 cup breadcrumbs
- 1/4 cup milk
- 1 small onion, finely chopped
- 1 tablespoon fresh parsley, chopped
- 1 egg
- Salt and pepper to taste

For the Soup:

- 6 cups clear beef or vegetable broth
- 1 carrot, finely diced
- 1 celery stalk, finely diced
- 1 leek, sliced
- 2 tablespoons butter
- Salt and pepper to taste
- Chopped fresh chives for garnish

Directions:

For the Liver Dumplings:

1. In a bowl, mix finely chopped liver, breadcrumbs, milk, chopped onion, chopped parsley, egg, salt, and pepper.
2. Form small dumplings from the mixture, about 1 inch in diameter.
3. Bring a pot of water to a gentle simmer and cook the liver dumplings for 10-15 minutes until cooked through. Remove and set aside.

For the Soup:

1. In a pot, sauté finely diced carrot, celery, and sliced leek in butter until softened.
2. Pour in the clear beef or vegetable broth and bring it to a gentle simmer.
3. Season with salt and pepper to taste.
4. Add the cooked liver dumplings to the simmering broth.
5. Cook for an additional 5 minutes until the dumplings are heated through.
6. Garnish with chopped fresh chives before serving.

Kürbiscremesuppe (Pumpkin Cream Soup)

Servings: 4

Time: 45 minutes

Ingredients:

- 1 medium-sized pumpkin, peeled, seeded, and diced (about 4 cups)
- 1 onion, chopped
- 2 cloves garlic, minced
- 2 tablespoons olive oil
- 4 cups vegetable or chicken broth
- 1 teaspoon ground cumin
- 1/2 teaspoon ground coriander
- Salt and pepper to taste
- 1 cup heavy cream
- Pumpkin seeds and fresh parsley for garnish

Directions:

1. In a large pot, heat olive oil over medium heat. Add chopped onion and garlic, sauté until softened.
2. Add diced pumpkin to the pot, stirring for about 5 minutes.

3. Pour in vegetable or chicken broth, ground cumin, ground coriander, salt, and pepper. Bring to a boil, then reduce heat and simmer until the pumpkin is tender.
4. Use an immersion blender to puree the soup until smooth. Alternatively, transfer the soup to a blender in batches.
5. Return the soup to the heat and stir in the heavy cream. Simmer for an additional 5 minutes.
6. Adjust seasoning if necessary.
7. Serve hot, garnished with pumpkin seeds and fresh parsley.

Krautsuppe (Cabbage Soup)

Servings: 6

Time: 45 minutes

Ingredients:

- 1/2 head green cabbage, shredded
- 1 onion, finely chopped
- 2 carrots, peeled and diced
- 2 potatoes, peeled and diced
- 1 leek, sliced
- 2 tablespoons vegetable oil
- 6 cups vegetable or beef broth
- 1 bay leaf
- 1 teaspoon caraway seeds
- Salt and pepper to taste
- Chopped fresh dill for garnish

Directions:

1. In a large pot, heat vegetable oil over medium heat. Add chopped onion and sauté until translucent.
2. Add shredded cabbage, diced carrots, diced potatoes, and sliced leek to the pot. Sauté for 5 minutes.
3. Pour in vegetable or beef broth, add a bay leaf, and sprinkle caraway seeds. Bring to a boil.

4. Reduce heat to low, cover, and simmer for about 30 minutes or until the vegetables are tender.
5. Season the soup with salt and pepper to taste.
6. Discard the bay leaf.
7. Serve hot, garnished with chopped fresh dill.

Steirische Eierschwammerlsuppe (Styrian Chanterelle Soup)

Servings: 4

Time: 40 minutes

Ingredients:

- 1 lb (about 450g) fresh chanterelle mushrooms, cleaned and chopped
- 1 onion, finely chopped
- 2 tablespoons butter
- 2 tablespoons all-purpose flour
- 4 cups chicken or vegetable broth
- 1 cup potatoes, peeled and diced
- 1/2 cup carrots, peeled and diced
- 1/2 cup celery, diced
- 1 cup milk
- Salt and pepper to taste
- Chopped fresh parsley for garnish

Directions:

1. In a large pot, melt butter over medium heat. Add chopped onion and sauté until translucent.
2. Add cleaned and chopped chanterelle mushrooms to the pot. Sauté for about 5 minutes.

3. Sprinkle flour over the mushroom mixture and stir well to create a roux.
4. Pour in chicken or vegetable broth, stirring continuously to avoid lumps.
5. Add diced potatoes, diced carrots, and diced celery to the pot. Bring to a simmer and cook until the vegetables are tender.
6. Stir in milk and let the soup simmer for an additional 10 minutes.
7. Season with salt and pepper to taste.
8. Serve hot, garnished with chopped fresh parsley.

Würstelgulasch (Sausage Goulash)

Servings: 4

Time: 40 minutes

Ingredients:

- 8 sausages of your choice (e.g., Vienna sausages, bratwurst), sliced
- 1 large onion, finely chopped
- 2 tablespoons vegetable oil
- 2 tablespoons sweet paprika
- 1 teaspoon caraway seeds
- 2 tablespoons tomato paste
- 1 red bell pepper, diced
- 2 cups beef broth
- Salt and pepper to taste
- Chopped fresh parsley for garnish

Directions:

1. In a large pot, heat vegetable oil over medium heat. Add chopped onion and sauté until translucent.
2. Add sliced sausages to the pot and cook until browned on all sides.
3. Stir in sweet paprika, caraway seeds, and tomato paste. Cook for 2 minutes.

4. Add diced red bell pepper to the pot and sauté for an additional 3-4 minutes.
5. Pour in beef broth, stirring to combine all ingredients.
6. Bring the goulash to a simmer and let it cook for about 20 minutes.
7. Season with salt and pepper to taste.
8. Serve hot, garnished with chopped fresh parsley.

Grammelknödel Suppe (Crackling Dumpling Soup)

Servings: 4

Time: 50 minutes

Ingredients:

For the Crackling Dumplings:

- 1 cup fresh white bread crumbs
- 1/2 cup milk
- 1/2 cup pork cracklings (Grammeln), finely chopped
- 1 small onion, finely chopped
- 2 tablespoons fresh parsley, chopped
- 2 eggs
- Salt and pepper to taste

For the Soup:

- 6 cups beef or vegetable broth
- 1 carrot, peeled and diced
- 1 leek, sliced
- 2 tablespoons butter
- Salt and pepper to taste
- Chopped fresh chives for garnish

Directions:

For the Crackling Dumplings:

1. In a bowl, combine fresh white bread crumbs and milk. Let it soak for a few minutes.
2. Add finely chopped pork cracklings, finely chopped onion, fresh parsley, eggs, salt, and pepper to the soaked bread crumbs. Mix well to form a dough.
3. Shape the dough into small dumplings, about 1 inch in diameter.

For the Soup:

1. In a pot, sauté diced carrot and sliced leek in butter until softened.
2. Pour in beef or vegetable broth and bring it to a gentle simmer.
3. Add the crackling dumplings to the simmering broth.
4. Cook for about 15-20 minutes until the dumplings are cooked through.
5. Season the soup with salt and pepper to taste.
6. Garnish with chopped fresh chives before serving.

Rindsuppe mit Frittaten (Beef Broth with Pancakes)

Servings: 4

Time: 30 minutes

Ingredients:

For the Pancakes:

- 1 cup all-purpose flour
- 2 eggs
- 1 cup milk
- Pinch of salt

For the Soup:

- 6 cups beef broth
- 1 carrot, julienned
- 1 leek, sliced
- Salt and pepper to taste
- Chopped fresh parsley for garnish

Directions:

For the Pancakes:

1. In a bowl, whisk together flour, eggs, milk, and a pinch of salt until smooth.

2. Heat a non-stick pan and pour a thin layer of batter. Cook until the pancake is set, then flip and cook the other side. Repeat until all batter is used.
3. Let the pancakes cool and then roll them up. Slice into thin strips.

For the Soup:

1. In a pot, bring beef broth to a simmer.
2. Add julienned carrot and sliced leek to the simmering broth. Cook until the vegetables are tender.
3. Season with salt and pepper to taste.
4. Add the sliced pancake strips to the simmering broth.
5. Cook for an additional 2-3 minutes until the strips are heated through.
6. Garnish with chopped fresh parsley before serving.

Karfiolcremesuppe (Cauliflower Cream Soup)

Servings: 4

Time: 30 minutes

Ingredients:

- 1 medium-sized cauliflower, chopped
- 1 onion, finely chopped
- 2 cloves garlic, minced
- 2 tablespoons butter
- 4 cups vegetable or chicken broth
- 1 cup milk
- 1/2 cup heavy cream
- Salt and pepper to taste
- Pinch of nutmeg (optional)
- Chopped fresh chives for garnish

Directions:

1. In a large pot, melt butter over medium heat. Add chopped onion and minced garlic, sauté until softened.
2. Add chopped cauliflower to the pot and cook for about 5 minutes.
3. Pour in vegetable or chicken broth, bring to a boil, then reduce heat and simmer until the cauliflower is tender.

4. Use an immersion blender to puree the soup until smooth. Alternatively, transfer the soup to a blender in batches.
5. Return the pureed soup to the heat, stir in milk and heavy cream.
6. Season with salt and pepper to taste. Add a pinch of nutmeg if desired.
7. Simmer for an additional 5 minutes to let the flavors meld.
8. Serve hot, garnished with chopped fresh chives.

MAIN COURSES - MEAT DISHES

Wiener Schnitzel

Servings: 4

Time: 30 minutes

Ingredients:

- 4 veal or pork cutlets, pounded thin
- Salt and pepper to taste
- 1 cup all-purpose flour
- 2 large eggs, beaten
- 1 cup breadcrumbs
- Vegetable oil for frying
- Lemon wedges for serving
- Fresh parsley for garnish

Directions:

1. Season the veal or pork cutlets with salt and pepper on both sides.
2. Set up a breading station with three shallow dishes: one with flour, one with beaten eggs, and one with breadcrumbs.
3. Dredge each cutlet in flour, shaking off excess.
4. Dip the cutlet into the beaten eggs, ensuring even coating.
5. Press the cutlet into breadcrumbs, making sure it is fully coated.
6. Heat vegetable oil in a large pan over medium-high heat.
7. Fry the cutlets for 3-4 minutes per side or until golden brown and cooked through.
8. Place the schnitzels on a paper towel to absorb excess oil.
9. Garnish with fresh parsley and serve hot with lemon wedges on the side.

Tafelspitz (Boiled Beef)

Servings: 4

Time: 2 hours

Ingredients:

- 2.5 lbs (about 1.2 kg) beef sirloin or rump roast
- Salt and pepper to taste
- 1 large onion, peeled and halved
- 2 carrots, peeled and halved
- 1 leek, cleaned and halved
- 1 celery stalk, halved
- 2 bay leaves
- 6-8 whole peppercorns
- Fresh parsley for garnish

Directions:

1. Place the beef roast in a large pot and cover it with cold water.
2. Season the water with salt and add the halved onion, carrots, leek, celery, bay leaves, and peppercorns.
3. Bring the water to a boil over high heat, then reduce the heat to low and let it simmer for about 1.5 to 2 hours, or until the beef is tender.
4. Occasionally skim off any foam that rises to the surface.

5. Once the beef is tender, remove it from the pot and let it rest for a few minutes.
6. Slice the beef into thin slices against the grain.
7. Strain the broth and discard the vegetables and spices.
8. Serve the sliced beef on a platter, garnished with fresh parsley.
9. Serve the clear broth in bowls on the side.

Schweinsbraten (Roast Pork)

Servings: 6

Time: 3 hours

Ingredients:

- 3 lbs (about 1.4kg) pork shoulder or pork loin roast
- Salt and pepper to taste
- 2 tablespoons vegetable oil
- 1 onion, chopped
- 2 cloves garlic, minced
- 2 tablespoons caraway seeds
- 1 tablespoon marjoram
- 1 cup beef or vegetable broth
- 1/2 cup dry white wine
- 2 tablespoons all-purpose flour (for gravy)
- Water (as needed for gravy)

Directions:

1. Preheat the oven to 350°F (175°C).
2. Score the skin of the pork roast with a sharp knife and season generously with salt and pepper.
3. In a large oven-safe pot or roasting pan, heat vegetable oil over medium-high heat.
4. Brown the pork roast on all sides until golden brown.

5. Add chopped onion and minced garlic to the pot, sautéing until softened.
6. Sprinkle caraway seeds and marjoram over the pork roast.
7. Pour in beef or vegetable broth and white wine.
8. Cover the pot and transfer it to the preheated oven.
9. Roast for about 2.5 to 3 hours or until the pork is cooked through and tender.
10. Remove the pork from the pot and let it rest before slicing.
11. For gravy: In a small pan, mix flour with water to create a smooth paste. Add it to the drippings in the pot and cook until thickened, stirring constantly.
12. Serve the sliced Schweinsbraten with the flavorful gravy.

Beuschel (Tripe Stew)

Servings: 4

Time: 3 hours

Ingredients:

- 1 lb (about 450g) tripe, cleaned and cut into small strips
- 1 calf's lung, cleaned and diced (optional, can be omitted)
- 1 onion, finely chopped
- 2 tablespoons vegetable oil
- 2 tablespoons all-purpose flour
- 1 cup white wine
- 4 cups beef or vegetable broth
- 1 teaspoon dried marjoram
- 1 teaspoon dried thyme
- Salt and pepper to taste
- Lemon juice to taste
- Chopped fresh parsley for garnish

Directions:

1. In a large pot, heat vegetable oil over medium heat. Add finely chopped onion and sauté until translucent.
2. Add tripe and calf's lung (if using) to the pot, cooking until lightly browned.
3. Sprinkle all-purpose flour over the tripe and stir to coat.

4. Pour in white wine, scraping the bottom of the pot to deglaze.
5. Add beef or vegetable broth, dried marjoram, and dried thyme to the pot. Bring to a boil.
6. Reduce the heat to low, cover, and simmer for about 2 to 2.5 hours or until the tripe is tender.
7. Season with salt, pepper, and lemon juice to taste.
8. Garnish with chopped fresh parsley before serving.

Hühnerfrikassee (Chicken Fricassee)

Servings: 4

Time: 1.5 hours

Ingredients:

- 1 whole chicken, cut into parts
- Salt and pepper to taste
- 2 tablespoons vegetable oil
- 1 onion, finely chopped
- 2 carrots, peeled and sliced
- 2 celery stalks, sliced
- 1 leek, sliced
- 1/4 cup all-purpose flour
- 2 cups chicken broth
- 1 cup heavy cream
- 1 teaspoon Dijon mustard
- 1 teaspoon lemon juice
- Fresh parsley for garnish

Directions:

1. Season chicken parts with salt and pepper.
2. In a large pot, heat vegetable oil over medium-high heat. Brown the chicken on all sides. Remove and set aside.

3. In the same pot, add chopped onion, sliced carrots, sliced celery, and sliced leek. Sauté until vegetables are softened.
4. Sprinkle all-purpose flour over the vegetables and stir to create a roux.
5. Slowly add chicken broth, stirring continuously to avoid lumps.
6. Return the browned chicken to the pot. Cover and simmer for about 45 minutes or until the chicken is cooked through.
7. In a separate bowl, mix heavy cream, Dijon mustard, and lemon juice.
8. Pour the cream mixture into the pot, stirring well. Simmer for an additional 10-15 minutes.
9. Adjust seasoning with salt and pepper to taste.
10. Garnish with fresh parsley before serving.

Zwiebelrostbraten (Onion Roast Beef)

Servings: 4

Time: 2 hours

Ingredients:

- 2 lbs (about 900g) beef sirloin or ribeye steaks
- Salt and pepper to taste
- 2 tablespoons vegetable oil
- 2 large onions, thinly sliced
- 1 tablespoon butter
- 1 cup beef broth
- 1 tablespoon all-purpose flour
- 1 teaspoon mustard (Dijon or whole grain)
- Chopped fresh parsley for garnish

Directions:

1. Preheat the oven to 350°F (175°C).
2. Season the beef steaks with salt and pepper on both sides.
3. In an oven-safe skillet, heat vegetable oil over medium-high heat. Sear the steaks until browned on both sides. Remove and set aside.
4. In the same skillet, add butter and thinly sliced onions. Sauté until the onions are golden brown.

5. Sprinkle flour over the onions and stir to create a roux.
6. Gradually add beef broth, stirring continuously to avoid lumps.
7. Stir in mustard and bring the mixture to a simmer.
8. Return the seared steaks to the skillet, coating them with the onion and broth mixture.
9. Transfer the skillet to the preheated oven and roast for about 30-40 minutes or until the beef reaches your desired doneness.
10. Baste the steaks with the onion and broth mixture during roasting.
11. Garnish with chopped fresh parsley before serving.

Leberkäse (Liver Cheese)

Servings: 8

Time: 2 hours

Ingredients:

- 1 lb (about 450g) pork shoulder, finely ground
- 1/2 lb (about 225g) pork liver, finely ground
- 1 cup ice-cold water
- 1 cup ice cubes
- 1 cup bread crumbs
- 1 small onion, finely chopped
- 1 teaspoon salt
- 1/2 teaspoon white pepper
- 1/4 teaspoon ground caraway seeds (optional)
- Butter or oil for greasing the pan

Directions:

1. Preheat the oven to 350°F (175°C).
2. In a large bowl, combine finely ground pork shoulder, finely ground pork liver, and ice-cold water.
3. Gradually add ice cubes to the mixture, stirring continuously until well combined.

4. Add bread crumbs, finely chopped onion, salt, white pepper, and ground caraway seeds (if using). Mix thoroughly.
5. Grease a loaf pan or a rectangular baking dish with butter or oil.
6. Pour the mixture into the prepared pan, ensuring it is evenly distributed.
7. Bake in the preheated oven for about 1.5 to 2 hours or until the top is golden brown and the center is cooked through.
8. Let the Leberkäse cool slightly before slicing.

Geselchtes mit Sauerkraut (Smoked Meat with Sauerkraut)

Servings: 6

Time: 2.5 hours

Ingredients:

- 2 lbs (about 900g) smoked pork belly or shoulder
- 1 onion, chopped
- 2 cloves garlic, minced
- 2 tablespoons vegetable oil
- 1 teaspoon caraway seeds
- 1 teaspoon juniper berries
- 1 bay leaf
- 1 large can (about 32 oz or 900g) sauerkraut, drained and rinsed
- 1 cup dry white wine
- Salt and pepper to taste
- Fresh parsley for garnish

Directions:

1. In a large pot or Dutch oven, heat vegetable oil over medium heat. Add chopped onion and sauté until translucent.

2. Add minced garlic, caraway seeds, juniper berries, and bay leaf to the pot. Sauté for an additional 2 minutes.
3. Place the smoked pork in the pot, searing it on all sides until browned.
4. Pour in dry white wine, scraping the bottom of the pot to deglaze.
5. Add drained and rinsed sauerkraut to the pot, mixing it with the other ingredients.
6. Season with salt and pepper to taste.
7. Cover the pot and let it simmer over low heat for about 2 hours, or until the smoked meat is tender and the flavors meld.
8. Garnish with fresh parsley before serving.

Rindsrouladen (Beef Rouladen)

Servings: 4

Time: 2 hours

Ingredients:

- 4 beef round steaks, thinly sliced
- Salt and pepper to taste
- Dijon mustard
- 4 slices bacon
- 1 onion, finely chopped
- 4 medium-sized pickles, sliced into thin strips
- 2 tablespoons vegetable oil
- 2 cups beef broth
- 1 cup dry red wine
- 2 tablespoons tomato paste
- 2 tablespoons all-purpose flour
- Fresh parsley for garnish

Directions:

1. Preheat the oven to 350°F (175°C).
2. Season each beef round steak with salt and pepper.
3. Spread a thin layer of Dijon mustard over each steak.
4. Place a slice of bacon on each steak, followed by a portion of finely chopped onion and pickle strips.

5. Roll up the steaks and secure with toothpicks or kitchen twine.
6. In a large skillet, heat vegetable oil over medium-high heat. Brown the beef rolls on all sides.
7. Transfer the browned rouladen to an ovenproof dish.
8. In the same skillet, add beef broth, dry red wine, and tomato paste. Bring to a simmer.
9. Pour the liquid over the rouladen in the ovenproof dish.
10. Cover the dish and bake in the preheated oven for about 1.5 hours or until the beef is tender.
11. Remove the rouladen from the dish and keep warm.
12. In a small bowl, mix all-purpose flour with a little water to create a smooth paste. Stir the paste into the liquid in the skillet to thicken the sauce.
13. Pour the thickened sauce over the rouladen.
14. Garnish with fresh parsley before serving.

Blunzengröstl (Blood Sausage Hash)

Servings: 4

Time: 40 minutes

Ingredients:

- 1 lb (about 450g) blood sausage, casing removed and crumbled
- 4 cups boiled potatoes, diced
- 1 large onion, finely chopped
- 2 tablespoons vegetable oil
- Salt and pepper to taste
- Chopped fresh chives for garnish
- Fried eggs (optional, for serving)

Directions:

1. In a large skillet, heat vegetable oil over medium heat. Add chopped onion and sauté until translucent.
2. Add crumbled blood sausage to the skillet, breaking it apart with a spoon. Cook until browned.
3. Add diced boiled potatoes to the skillet, stirring to combine with the sausage and onion.
4. Season with salt and pepper to taste. Cook until the potatoes are crispy and browned.
5. Garnish with chopped fresh chives.

6. Optionally, serve Blunzengröstl with fried eggs on top.

MAIN COURSES - VEGETARIAN DISHES

Kasnocken (Cheese Dumplings)

Servings: 4

Time: 30 minutes

Ingredients:

- 2 cups all-purpose flour
- 3 large eggs
- 1/2 cup water
- 1/2 teaspoon salt
- 1 cup shredded mountain cheese (such as Emmental or Gruyère)
- 1/2 cup chopped chives or green onions

- Butter for frying
- Freshly ground black pepper to taste

Directions:

1. In a large bowl, whisk together flour, eggs, water, and salt to form a smooth batter.
2. Stir in shredded mountain cheese and chopped chives or green onions until evenly distributed.
3. Bring a large pot of salted water to a boil.
4. Using a spaetzle maker or a coarse grater, drop small portions of the batter into the boiling water, forming small dumplings. Cook for 2-3 minutes or until they float to the surface.
5. Use a slotted spoon to transfer the Kasnocken to a colander, draining excess water.
6. In a large skillet, melt butter over medium heat. Add the boiled Kasnocken to the skillet, frying until golden brown.
7. Season with freshly ground black pepper to taste.

Spinatknödel (Spinach Dumplings)

Servings: 4

Time: 45 minutes

Ingredients:

- 1 lb (about 450g) fresh spinach, washed and chopped
- 1 1/2 cups breadcrumbs
- 1/2 cup milk
- 1/2 cup all-purpose flour
- 2 tablespoons butter
- 1 small onion, finely chopped
- 2 eggs
- Salt and pepper to taste
- Nutmeg to taste
- Grated Parmesan cheese for garnish
- Butter for serving

Directions:

1. In a large pot, steam or sauté the chopped spinach until wilted. Drain and let it cool.
2. In a pan, melt 2 tablespoons of butter and sauté the finely chopped onion until translucent.

3. In a bowl, combine the chopped spinach, sautéed onion, breadcrumbs, milk, flour, eggs, salt, pepper, and a pinch of nutmeg. Mix until well combined.
4. Let the mixture rest for 10-15 minutes to allow the breadcrumbs to absorb the liquid.
5. Form the mixture into round dumplings, about the size of a golf ball.
6. Bring a large pot of salted water to a simmer.
7. Carefully drop the dumplings into the simmering water. Cook for about 15-20 minutes or until they float to the surface.
8. Use a slotted spoon to remove the dumplings and drain any excess water.
9. Serve the Spinatknödel hot, garnished with grated Parmesan cheese and a drizzle of melted butter.

Schwammerlgulasch (Mushroom Goulash)

Servings: 4

Time: 40 minutes

Ingredients:

- 1 lb (about 450g) mixed mushrooms (such as button, cremini, and shiitake), sliced
- 2 onions, finely chopped
- 2 cloves garlic, minced
- 2 tablespoons vegetable oil
- 2 tablespoons tomato paste
- 1 tablespoon sweet paprika
- 1 teaspoon caraway seeds
- 1 teaspoon marjoram
- 1 cup vegetable broth
- 1/2 cup dry red wine
- Salt and pepper to taste
- Chopped fresh parsley for garnish
- Sour cream for serving (optional)

Directions:

1. In a large pot or Dutch oven, heat vegetable oil over medium heat. Add finely chopped onions and sauté until translucent.

2. Add minced garlic and sliced mushrooms to the pot, cooking until the mushrooms release their moisture.
3. Stir in tomato paste, sweet paprika, caraway seeds, and marjoram. Cook for an additional 2 minutes.
4. Pour in vegetable broth and red wine. Bring the mixture to a simmer.
5. Reduce the heat to low, cover the pot, and let it simmer for about 20-25 minutes, allowing the flavors to meld.
6. Season with salt and pepper to taste.
7. Garnish with chopped fresh parsley before serving.
8. Optionally, serve Schwammerlgulasch with a dollop of sour cream.

Käsekrainer mit Sauerkraut (Cheese-filled Sausages with Sauerkraut)

Servings: 4

Time: 30 minutes

Ingredients:

- 4 Käsekrainer sausages (cheese-filled sausages)
- 1 lb (about 450g) sauerkraut, drained and rinsed
- 1 tablespoon vegetable oil
- 1 onion, finely chopped
- 2 cloves garlic, minced
- 1 teaspoon caraway seeds
- 1 cup dry white wine
- Salt and pepper to taste
- Mustard for serving

Directions:

1. In a large skillet, heat vegetable oil over medium heat. Add finely chopped onion and sauté until translucent.
2. Add minced garlic and caraway seeds to the skillet, cooking for an additional 2 minutes.
3. Add drained and rinsed sauerkraut to the skillet, stirring to combine with the onion mixture.

4. Pour in dry white wine and let it simmer for about 10-15 minutes or until the sauerkraut is tender.
5. Meanwhile, grill or pan-fry the Käsekrainer sausages until they are cooked through and have a golden-brown exterior.
6. Season the sauerkraut with salt and pepper to taste.
7. Serve the Käsekrainer sausages hot in a bed of sauerkraut.
8. Optionally, serve with mustard on the side.

Erdäpfelgulasch (Potato Goulash)

Servings: 4

Time: 40 minutes

Ingredients:

- 4 large potatoes, peeled and diced
- 2 onions, finely chopped
- 2 cloves garlic, minced
- 2 tablespoons vegetable oil
- 2 tablespoons tomato paste
- 2 tablespoons sweet paprika
- 1 teaspoon caraway seeds
- 1 teaspoon marjoram
- 4 cups vegetable broth
- Salt and pepper to taste
- Chopped fresh parsley for garnish

Directions:

1. In a large pot or Dutch oven, heat vegetable oil over medium heat. Add finely chopped onions and sauté until translucent.
2. Add minced garlic, diced potatoes, tomato paste, sweet paprika, caraway seeds, and marjoram to the pot. Stir to coat the potatoes with the spices.

3. Pour in vegetable broth, ensuring the potatoes are fully covered. Bring the mixture to a simmer.
4. Reduce the heat to low, cover the pot, and let it simmer for about 20-25 minutes or until the potatoes are tender.
5. Season with salt and pepper to taste.
6. Garnish with chopped fresh parsley before serving.

Gemüsestrudel (Vegetable Strudel)

Servings: 4-6

Time: 1 hour

Ingredients:

For the Filling:

- 2 tablespoons olive oil
- 1 onion, finely chopped
- 2 cloves garlic, minced
- 1 zucchini, diced
- 1 red bell pepper, diced
- 1 yellow bell pepper, diced
- 1 carrot, grated
- 1 cup mushrooms, sliced
- Salt and pepper to taste
- 1 teaspoon dried oregano
- 1 teaspoon dried thyme
- 1 cup grated cheese (Gouda or Swiss)

For the Strudel:

- 10 sheets phyllo pastry
- 1/2 cup unsalted butter, melted

Directions:

For the Filling:

1. In a large pan, heat olive oil over medium heat. Add chopped onion and sauté until translucent.
2. Add minced garlic and sauté for an additional minute.
3. Add diced zucchini, red bell pepper, yellow bell pepper, grated carrot, and sliced mushrooms to the pan. Cook until the vegetables are tender.
4. Season with salt, pepper, dried oregano, and dried thyme. Stir to combine.
5. Remove the pan from heat and let the vegetable mixture cool.
6. Once cooled, stir in grated cheese.

For the Strudel:

1. Preheat the oven to 375°F (190°C).
2. Place one sheet of phyllo pastry on a clean surface and brush it lightly with melted butter. Repeat with the remaining sheets, stacking them on top of each other.
3. Spoon the vegetable and cheese filling along one edge of the phyllo stack.
4. Roll the phyllo stack over the filling to form a log or cylinder.
5. Place the rolled strudel on a baking sheet lined with parchment paper, seam side down.

6. Brush the top of the strudel with melted butter.
7. Bake in the preheated oven for about 25-30 minutes or until the strudel is golden brown and crisp.
8. Remove from the oven and let it cool for a few minutes before slicing.

Kürbisrisotto (Pumpkin Risotto)

Servings: 4

Time: 30 minutes

Ingredients:

- 1 1/2 cups Arborio rice
- 1 small pumpkin (about 2 cups), peeled, seeded, and diced
- 1 onion, finely chopped
- 2 cloves garlic, minced
- 4 cups vegetable broth, kept warm
- 1 cup dry white wine
- 1/2 cup Parmesan cheese, grated
- 2 tablespoons butter
- 2 tablespoons olive oil
- Salt and pepper to taste
- Fresh parsley for garnish

Directions:

1. In a large skillet or pan, heat olive oil over medium heat. Add finely chopped onion and sauté until translucent.
2. Add minced garlic and Arborio rice to the skillet, stirring to coat the rice with oil.

3. Pour in dry white wine, stirring constantly until it's mostly absorbed by the rice.
4. Add diced pumpkin to the skillet and continue stirring.
5. Begin adding the warm vegetable broth, one ladle at a time, allowing the liquid to be absorbed before adding more. Stir continuously.
6. Continue this process until the rice is creamy and cooked to al dente, which will take about 18-20 minutes.
7. Stir in grated Parmesan cheese and butter. Season with salt and pepper to taste.
8. Remove from heat, cover, and let it rest for a few minutes.
9. Garnish with fresh parsley before serving.

Topfenknödel (Quark Dumplings)

Servings: 4

Time: 40 minutes

Ingredients:

For the Dumplings:

- 1 cup Quark (curd cheese or farmer cheese)
- 2 cups dry bread crumbs
- 2 large eggs
- 1/4 cup unsalted butter, melted
- 1/4 cup granulated sugar
- 1 teaspoon vanilla extract
- 1/2 teaspoon baking powder
- Pinch of salt
- All-purpose flour for dusting

For the Vanilla Sauce:

- 2 cups milk
- 1/2 cup granulated sugar
- 1 vanilla bean or 1 teaspoon vanilla extract
- 2 tablespoons cornstarch

Directions:

For the Dumplings:

1. In a large bowl, combine Quark, dry bread crumbs, eggs, melted butter, granulated sugar, vanilla extract, baking powder, and a pinch of salt. Mix well until a smooth dough forms.
2. Let the dough rest for about 15 minutes.
3. Bring a large pot of water to a simmer with a pinch of salt.
4. With floured hands, form the dough into small, round dumplings.
5. Gently place the dumplings into the simmering water. Cook for about 15 minutes or until they float to the surface.
6. Remove the dumplings with a slotted spoon and let them drain briefly.

For the Vanilla Sauce:

1. In a saucepan, heat milk over medium heat. If using a vanilla bean, split it open and scrape the seeds into the milk. Add the whole bean to infuse.
2. In a bowl, whisk together granulated sugar and cornstarch.
3. Gradually whisk the sugar and cornstarch mixture into the warm milk.
4. Continue to whisk and cook until the sauce thickens.
5. If using vanilla extract, add it to the sauce.

TRADITIONAL AUSTRIAN COOKBOOK

Krautfleisch (Cabbage and Meat Stew)

Servings: 4

Time: 2 hours

Ingredients:

- 1 lb (about 450g) beef stew meat, cubed
- 1 large cabbage, shredded
- 2 onions, finely chopped
- 2 cloves garlic, minced
- 2 tablespoons vegetable oil
- 1 tablespoon tomato paste
- 2 teaspoons sweet paprika
- 1 teaspoon caraway seeds
- 2 bay leaves
- 2 cups beef broth
- Salt and pepper to taste
- Chopped fresh parsley for garnish

Directions:

1. In a large pot or Dutch oven, heat vegetable oil over medium heat. Add finely chopped onions and sauté until translucent.
2. Add minced garlic and cubed beef stew meat to the pot, browning the meat on all sides.

3. Stir in tomato paste, sweet paprika, and caraway seeds. Cook for an additional 2 minutes.
4. Add shredded cabbage to the pot, mixing it with the other ingredients.
5. Pour in beef broth and add bay leaves. Bring the mixture to a simmer.
6. Cover the pot and let it simmer over low heat for about 1.5 to 2 hours, or until the meat is tender and the flavors meld.
7. Season with salt and pepper to taste.
8. Garnish with chopped fresh parsley before serving.

Linsen mit Knödel (Lentils with Dumplings)

Servings: 4

Time: 1 hour

Ingredients:

For the Lentils:

- 2 cups brown or green lentils, rinsed and drained
- 1 onion, finely chopped
- 2 carrots, diced
- 2 cloves garlic, minced
- 2 tablespoons vegetable oil
- 1 bay leaf
- 1 teaspoon dried thyme
- 4 cups vegetable broth
- Salt and pepper to taste
- Apple cider vinegar (optional, for serving)

For the Dumplings:

- 2 cups stale bread cubes
- 1/2 cup milk
- 2 eggs
- 1/4 cup all-purpose flour
- 1/4 cup butter, melted

- Salt and pepper to taste
- Chopped fresh parsley for garnish

Directions:

For the Lentils:

1. In a large pot or Dutch oven, heat vegetable oil over medium heat. Add finely chopped onions and sauté until translucent.
2. Add minced garlic and diced carrots to the pot, sautéing for an additional 2 minutes.
3. Stir in rinsed lentils, bay leaf, dried thyme, and vegetable broth. Bring the mixture to a boil.
4. Reduce the heat to low, cover the pot, and let it simmer for about 25-30 minutes or until the lentils are tender.
5. Season with salt and pepper to taste.
6. If desired, add a splash of apple cider vinegar just before serving.

For the Dumplings:

1. In a bowl, soak stale bread cubes in milk until softened.
2. Add eggs, all-purpose flour, melted butter, salt, and pepper to the soaked bread cubes. Mix until well combined.

3. Let the mixture rest for 10-15 minutes to allow the bread to absorb the liquid.
4. With floured hands, form the mixture into round dumplings.

DESSERTS AND PASTRIES

Apfelstrudel (Apple Strudel)

Servings: 8

Time: 1 hour

Ingredients:

For the Strudel Dough:

- 2 cups all-purpose flour
- 1/2 cup lukewarm water
- 2 tablespoons vegetable oil
- 1 egg
- Pinch of salt

For the Filling:

- 6 medium-sized apples, peeled, cored, and thinly sliced
- 1 cup breadcrumbs
- 1 cup granulated sugar
- 1 teaspoon ground cinnamon
- 1/2 cup raisins (optional)
- 1/2 cup melted unsalted butter
- Powdered sugar for dusting

Directions:

For the Strudel Dough:

1. In a large bowl, combine flour and a pinch of salt. Make a well in the center.
2. In a separate bowl, mix lukewarm water, vegetable oil, and egg. Pour this mixture into the well of the flour.
3. Knead the dough until smooth and elastic. Cover and let it rest for about 30 minutes.

For the Filling:

1. Preheat the oven to 375°F (190°C).
2. Roll out the strudel dough on a floured surface until very thin.
3. Sprinkle breadcrumbs evenly over the rolled-out dough.
4. Arrange the thinly sliced apples over the breadcrumbs.

5. In a small bowl, mix granulated sugar and ground cinnamon. Sprinkle this mixture over the apples. Add raisins if desired.
6. Drizzle melted butter over the entire filling.
7. Carefully roll the strudel, tucking in the ends as you go. Place it seam-side down on a baking sheet.
8. Brush the top of the strudel with additional melted butter.
9. Bake in the preheated oven for about 30-35 minutes or until golden brown.
10. Let it cool slightly before dusting with powdered sugar.

Sachertorte (Sacher Cake)

Servings: 12

Time: 2 hours

Ingredients:

For the Cake:

- 1 cup (225g) unsalted butter, softened
- 1 cup granulated sugar
- 8 large eggs, separated
- 1 teaspoon vanilla extract
- 1 cup all-purpose flour
- 1 cup ground almonds
- 1/2 cup unsweetened cocoa powder
- 1 teaspoon baking powder
- Pinch of salt

For the Apricot Jam Filling:

- 1 cup apricot jam

For the Chocolate Glaze:

- 7 ounces (200g) dark chocolate, finely chopped
- 1 cup heavy cream
- 2 tablespoons unsalted butter

Directions:

For the Cake:

1. Preheat the oven to 350°F (175°C). Grease and flour a 9-inch (23 cm) round cake pan.
2. In a large bowl, cream together softened butter and granulated sugar until light and fluffy.
3. Add egg yolks one at a time, beating well after each addition. Stir in vanilla extract.
4. In a separate bowl, sift together flour, ground almonds, cocoa powder, baking powder, and a pinch of salt.
5. Gradually add the dry ingredients to the butter mixture, mixing until well combined.
6. In a clean, dry bowl, whip the egg whites until stiff peaks form. Gently fold the egg whites into the batter.
7. Pour the batter into the prepared cake pan and smooth the top.
8. Bake for about 45-50 minutes or until a toothpick inserted into the center comes out clean.
9. Allow the cake to cool in the pan for 10 minutes, then transfer it to a wire rack to cool completely.

For the Apricot Jam Filling:

1. Heat the apricot jam in a small saucepan until it becomes liquid.

2. Strain the jam to remove any chunks.

For the Chocolate Glaze:

1. Place finely chopped dark chocolate in a heatproof bowl.
2. In a small saucepan, heat the heavy cream until it begins to simmer. Pour the hot cream over the chocolate and let it sit for a minute.
3. Stir the chocolate and cream until smooth. Add unsalted butter and stir until well combined.

Assembly:

1. Cut the cooled cake in half horizontally to create two layers.
2. Spread a thin layer of strained apricot jam on the bottom layer.
3. Place the second layer on top and cover the entire cake with the chocolate glaze.
4. Allow the glaze to set before serving.

Topfenstrudel (Quark Strudel)

Servings: 6

Time: 1 hour

Ingredients:

For the Strudel Dough:

- 2 cups all-purpose flour
- 1/2 cup lukewarm water
- 2 tablespoons vegetable oil
- 1 egg
- Pinch of salt

For the Filling:

- 2 cups Quark (curd cheese or farmer cheese)
- 1/2 cup granulated sugar
- 2 tablespoons semolina or farina
- 1 teaspoon vanilla extract
- Zest of 1 lemon
- 1/2 cup raisins (optional)
- 1/4 cup melted unsalted butter
- Powdered sugar for dusting

Directions:

For the Strudel Dough:

1. In a large bowl, combine flour and a pinch of salt. Make a well in the center.
2. In a separate bowl, mix lukewarm water, vegetable oil, and egg. Pour this mixture into the well of the flour.
3. Knead the dough until smooth and elastic. Cover and let it rest for about 30 minutes.

For the Filling:

1. Preheat the oven to 375°F (190°C).
2. Roll out the strudel dough on a floured surface until very thin.
3. In a bowl, mix Quark, granulated sugar, semolina, vanilla extract, lemon zest, and raisins if desired.
4. Spread the Quark filling evenly over the rolled-out dough.
5. Drizzle melted butter over the filling.
6. Carefully roll the strudel, tucking in the ends as you go. Place it seam-side down on a baking sheet.
7. Brush the top of the strudel with additional melted butter.
8. Bake in the preheated oven for about 30-35 minutes or until golden brown.
9. Let it cool slightly before dusting with powdered sugar.

Kaiserschmarrn (Emperor's Pancake)

Servings: 4

Time: 30 minutes

Ingredients:

- 1 cup all-purpose flour
- 1 cup milk
- 4 large eggs, separated
- 2 tablespoons granulated sugar
- 1 teaspoon vanilla extract
- Pinch of salt
- 4 tablespoons unsalted butter
- Powdered sugar for dusting
- Jam or applesauce for serving (optional)

Directions:

1. In a bowl, whisk together flour, milk, egg yolks, sugar, vanilla extract, and a pinch of salt until you have a smooth batter.
2. In a separate bowl, beat egg whites until stiff peaks form.
3. Gently fold the beaten egg whites into the batter.
4. In a large non-stick skillet, melt 2 tablespoons of butter over medium heat.

5. Pour half of the batter into the skillet, spreading it evenly.
6. Cook until the bottom is golden brown, then flip and cook the other side until golden.
7. Tear the pancake into bite-sized pieces using two forks.
8. Repeat the process with the remaining batter, adding more butter as needed.
9. Dust the Kaiserschmarrn with powdered sugar before serving.
10. Optionally, serve with jam or applesauce on the side.

Dobostorte (Dobos Cake)

Servings: 12

Time: 2.5 hours

Ingredients:

For the Cake Layers:

- 6 large eggs, separated
- 1 cup granulated sugar
- 1 cup all-purpose flour
- 1 teaspoon baking powder
- 1/2 cup unsalted butter, melted and cooled
- 1 teaspoon vanilla extract

For the Chocolate Buttercream:

- 2 cups unsalted butter, softened
- 1 cup powdered sugar
- 8 oz (225g) bittersweet chocolate, melted and cooled

For the Caramel Topping:

- 1 cup granulated sugar
- 1/4 cup water
- 2 tablespoons unsalted butter

Directions:

For the Cake Layers:

1. Preheat the oven to 350°F (175°C). Grease and flour 6 (9-inch) cake pans.
2. In a large bowl, beat egg yolks and sugar until light and fluffy.
3. In a separate bowl, whisk together flour and baking powder. Gradually add the dry ingredients to the egg yolk mixture, mixing well.
4. Stir in melted butter and vanilla extract.
5. In another bowl, beat egg whites until stiff peaks form. Gently fold the egg whites into the batter.
6. Divide the batter equally among the prepared cake pans and smooth the tops.
7. Bake for about 8-10 minutes or until the edges are lightly golden. Repeat until all layers are baked.
8. Allow the cake layers to cool completely on wire racks.

For the Chocolate Buttercream:

1. In a bowl, beat softened butter until creamy.
2. Gradually add powdered sugar and continue to beat until light and fluffy.
3. Mix in melted and cooled bittersweet chocolate until well combined.

For the Caramel Topping:

1. In a saucepan, combine granulated sugar and water. Cook over medium heat without stirring until it turns into a deep amber color.
2. Remove from heat and stir in unsalted butter. Be cautious, as the mixture will bubble.
3. Pour the caramel onto a parchment-lined surface and let it cool and harden. Once cooled, break it into shards.

Assembling the Dobostorte:

1. Place one cake layer on a serving plate and spread a thin layer of chocolate buttercream on top.
2. Repeat the process, layering cake and chocolate buttercream.
3. Frost the entire cake with the remaining chocolate buttercream, creating a smooth surface.
4. Press the caramel shards onto the sides of the cake, creating a decorative pattern.
5. Optionally, pipe additional buttercream around the top edge of the cake.

Linzer Torte

Servings: 10

Time: 1.5 hours

Ingredients:

For the Dough:

- 1 cup unsalted butter, softened
- 1 cup granulated sugar
- 1 large egg
- 1 teaspoon vanilla extract
- 2 cups all-purpose flour
- 1 teaspoon ground cinnamon
- 1/2 teaspoon ground cloves
- 1/2 teaspoon baking powder
- 1/2 cup ground almonds or hazelnuts

For the Filling:

- 1 1/2 cups raspberry jam
- 1 cup ground almonds or hazelnuts

Directions:

1. Preheat the oven to 350°F (175°C). Grease and flour a 9-inch (23cm) tart pan with a removable bottom.

2. In a large bowl, cream together softened butter and granulated sugar until light and fluffy.
3. Beat in the egg and vanilla extract until well combined.
4. In a separate bowl, whisk together flour, ground cinnamon, ground cloves, baking powder, and ground almonds or hazelnuts.
5. Gradually add the dry ingredients to the wet ingredients, mixing until a soft dough forms.
6. Divide the dough in half. Press one half into the bottom and up the sides of the prepared tart pan.
7. Spread the raspberry jam evenly over the dough in the tart pan.
8. Mix the remaining ground almonds or hazelnuts into the remaining dough. Crumble this mixture over the raspberry jam.
9. Bake in the preheated oven for about 40-45 minutes or until the edges are golden brown.
10. Allow the Linzer Torte to cool completely in the tart pan before removing the sides.

Mohr im Hemd (Chocolate Pudding with Whipped Cream)

Servings: 4

Time: 1 hour

Ingredients:

For the Chocolate Pudding:

- 1 cup whole milk
- 1/2 cup granulated sugar
- 1/4 cup unsweetened cocoa powder
- 1/4 cup semolina or fine-grain cream of wheat
- 2 tablespoons unsalted butter
- 1 teaspoon vanilla extract
- A pinch of salt

For the Whipped Cream:

- 1 cup heavy cream
- 2 tablespoons powdered sugar
- 1 teaspoon vanilla extract

Directions:

For the Chocolate Pudding:

1. In a saucepan, combine milk, sugar, cocoa powder, semolina (or cream of wheat), and a pinch of salt.

2. Cook over medium heat, whisking constantly, until the mixture thickens and comes to a boil.
3. Remove from heat and stir in unsalted butter and vanilla extract until well combined.
4. Let the chocolate pudding cool slightly while preparing the whipped cream.

For the Whipped Cream:

1. In a chilled bowl, whip the heavy cream until it begins to thicken.
2. Add powdered sugar and vanilla extract, and continue whipping until stiff peaks form.

Assembling Mohr im Hemd:

1. Spoon the warm chocolate pudding into serving bowls or cups.
2. Top each serving with a generous dollop of whipped cream.

Nusskipferl (Nut Crescents)

Servings: 24 crescents

Time: 1.5 hours

Ingredients:

For the Dough:

- 2 cups all-purpose flour
- 1 cup unsalted butter, cold and cut into small pieces
- 1 cup ground walnuts or hazelnuts
- 1/2 cup granulated sugar
- 1 egg yolk
- 1 teaspoon vanilla extract
- A pinch of salt

For Coating:

- 1/2 cup powdered sugar

Directions:

1. Preheat the oven to 350°F (175°C). Line a baking sheet with parchment paper.
2. In a large bowl, combine all-purpose flour, cold butter pieces, ground nuts, granulated sugar, egg yolk, vanilla extract, and a pinch of salt.

3. Knead the ingredients together until a smooth dough forms. You can use a food processor for this step.
4. Divide the dough into smaller portions. Take one portion at a time and roll it into a log shape.
5. Cut the log into small pieces and shape each piece into a crescent shape.
6. Place the crescents on the prepared baking sheet, leaving some space between each.
7. Bake in the preheated oven for about 12-15 minutes or until the edges are lightly golden.
8. Allow the Nusskipferl to cool on the baking sheet for a few minutes before transferring them to a wire rack.

For Coating:

1. Once the Nusskipferl are completely cooled, roll them in powdered sugar until well coated.

Buchteln (Sweet Yeast Dumplings)

Servings: 12 dumplings

Time: 2.5 hours (includes rising time)

Ingredients:

For the Dough:

- 4 cups all-purpose flour
- 1/2 cup granulated sugar
- 1 packet (2 1/4 teaspoons) active dry yeast
- 1 cup warm milk (110°F/43°C)
- 1/2 cup unsalted butter, melted
- 2 large eggs
- 1 teaspoon vanilla extract
- A pinch of salt

For the Filling:

- 1/2 cup fruit jam (apricot or plum are traditional)
- Powdered sugar for dusting

Directions:

For the Dough:

1. In a small bowl, dissolve the yeast in warm milk and let it sit for 5 minutes until foamy.
2. In a large bowl, combine flour, sugar, and a pinch of salt.

3. Make a well in the center and add the yeast mixture, melted butter, eggs, and vanilla extract.
4. Mix the ingredients until a soft dough forms.
5. Turn the dough out onto a floured surface and knead for about 5-7 minutes until smooth and elastic.
6. Place the dough in a greased bowl, cover with a damp cloth, and let it rise in a warm place for about 1.5 to 2 hours, or until doubled in size.

Assembling Buchteln:

1. Preheat the oven to 350°F (175°C). Grease a baking dish.
2. Punch down the risen dough and divide it into 12 equal portions.
3. Roll each portion into a ball and flatten it with your hands.
4. Place a small spoonful of fruit jam in the center of each flattened dough portion.
5. Gather the edges of the dough and pinch them together to seal, forming a ball.
6. Place the filled dough balls in the prepared baking dish, with the sealed side down.
7. Let the filled dough balls rise for an additional 15-20 minutes.

Baking and Serving:

1. Bake in the preheated oven for 20-25 minutes or until the Buchteln are golden brown.
2. Dust with powdered sugar before serving.

Esterházytorte (Esterházy Cake)

Servings: 12

Time: 2 hours (includes chilling time)

Ingredients:

For the Cake Layers:

- 6 large eggs, separated
- 1 cup granulated sugar
- 1 1/2 cups ground almonds
- 1/2 cup all-purpose flour
- 1 teaspoon baking powder
- 1/2 teaspoon almond extract

For the Filling:

- 1 cup unsalted butter, softened
- 2 cups powdered sugar
- 1 teaspoon vanilla extract
- 1/2 cup ground almonds
- 1/2 cup finely chopped candied lemon peel

For the Glaze:

- 1 cup powdered sugar
- 2 tablespoons water
- 1 teaspoon lemon juice

Directions:

For the Cake Layers:

1. Preheat the oven to 350°F (175°C). Grease and flour three 9-inch (23cm) round cake pans.
2. In a large bowl, beat egg yolks and granulated sugar until light and fluffy.
3. In a separate bowl, whisk together ground almonds, all-purpose flour, and baking powder.
4. Gradually add the dry ingredients to the egg yolk mixture, mixing well.
5. Stir in almond extract.
6. In another bowl, beat egg whites until stiff peaks form. Gently fold the beaten egg whites into the batter.
7. Divide the batter evenly among the prepared cake pans and smooth the tops.
8. Bake for about 15-18 minutes or until the edges are lightly golden. Allow the cake layers to cool completely on wire racks.

For the Filling:

1. In a bowl, cream together softened butter, powdered sugar, and vanilla extract until smooth.
2. Stir in ground almonds and finely chopped candied lemon peel.

Assembling the Esterházytorte:

1. Place one cake layer on a serving plate and spread a generous portion of the filling over it.
2. Repeat the process, layering cake and filling.
3. Frost the top and sides of the cake with any remaining filling. Smooth the surface.

For the Glaze:

1. In a small bowl, whisk together powdered sugar, water, and lemon juice until smooth.
2. Drizzle the glaze over the top of the cake in a decorative pattern.

MEASURES

1. **Volume Conversions:**
   - 1 cup = 240 milliliters
   - 1 tablespoon = 15 milliliters
   - 1 teaspoon = 5 milliliters
   - 1 fluid ounce = 30 milliliters
2. **Weight Conversions:**
   - 1 ounce = 28 grams
   - 1 pound = 453 grams
   - 1 kilogram = 2.2 pounds
3. **Temperature Conversions:**
   - Celsius to Fahrenheit: $F = (C \times 9/5) + 32$
   - Fahrenheit to Celsius: $C = (F - 32) \times 5/9$
4. **Length Conversions:**
   - 1 inch = 2.54 centimeters

- 1 foot = 30.48 centimeters
- 1 meter = 39.37 inches

5. **Common Ingredient Conversions:**
- **1 stick of butter = 1/2 cup = 113 grams**
- **1 cup of flour = 120 grams**
- **1 cup of sugar = 200 grams**

6. **Oven Temperature Conversions:**
- **Gas Mark 1 = 275°F = 140°C**
- **Gas Mark 2 = 300°F = 150°C**
- **Gas Mark 4 = 350°F = 180°C**
- **Gas Mark 6 = 400°F = 200°C**
- **Gas Mark 8 = 450°F = 230°C.**

Printed in Great Britain
by Amazon